187227

PowerKids Readers:
The Bilingual Library of the
United States of America™

MARYLAND

VANESSA BROWN

TRADUCCIÓN AL ESPAÑOL: MARÍA CRISTINA BRUSCA

The Rosen Publishing Group's
PowerKids Press™ & **Editorial Buenas Letras**™
New York

Published in 2006 by The Rosen Publishing Group, Inc.
29 East 21st Street, New York, NY 10010

First Edition

Book Design: Albert B. Hanner
Photo Credits: Cover, pp. 9, 21, 30 (The Old Line State) © Lowell Georgia/Corbis; p. 5 Joseph Sohm; ChromeSohm Inc./Corbis; pp. 7, 26, 31 (Border) © Geoatlas; pp. 11, 31 (Ruth, Taussig) © Bettmann/Corbis; pp. 13, 17, 31 (Douglas, Tubman) © Corbis; pp. 15, 31 (Railroad) © Underwood & Underwood/ Corbis; p. 19 © Lynda Richardson/Corbis; pp. 23, 25, 30 (Capital, State Motto) © Richard T. Nowtz/Corbis; p. 30 (Black-eyed Susan) © Darrell Gulin/Corbis; p. 30 (Baltimore Oriole) © Arthur Morris/Corbis; p. 30 (White Oak) © Richard Hamilton Smith/Corbis; p. 31 (Glass) © S.I.N./Corbis; p. 31 (Ripkin Jr.) © Reuters/Corbis; p. 31 (Seafood) © Bob Krist/Corbis

Library of Congress Cataloging-in-Publication Data

Brown, Vanessa, 1963–
Maryland / Vanessa Brown ; traducción al español, María Cristina Brusca.—1st ed.
p. cm. — (The bilingual library of the United States of America) English and Spanish
Includes bibliographical references (p.) and index.
ISBN 1-4042-3085-8 (lib. bdg.)
1. Maryland—Juvenile literature. I. Title. II. Series.
F181.3.B76 2006
975.2–dc22
                                                                2005008350

Manufactured in the United States of America

Due to the changing nature of Internet links, Editorial Buenas Letras has developed an online list of Web sites related to the subject of this book. This site is updated regularly. Please use this link to access the list:

http://www.buenasletraslinks.com/ls/maryland

Contents

Contenido

Maryland Geography

Maryland borders Delaware, Pennsylvania, West Virginia, Virginia, and the District of Columbia. The Chesapeake Bay is in Maryland.

Geografía de Maryland

Maryland linda con Delaware, Pensilvania, Virginia, Virginia Occidental y el Distrito de Columbia. La Bahía Chesapeake se encuentra en Maryland.

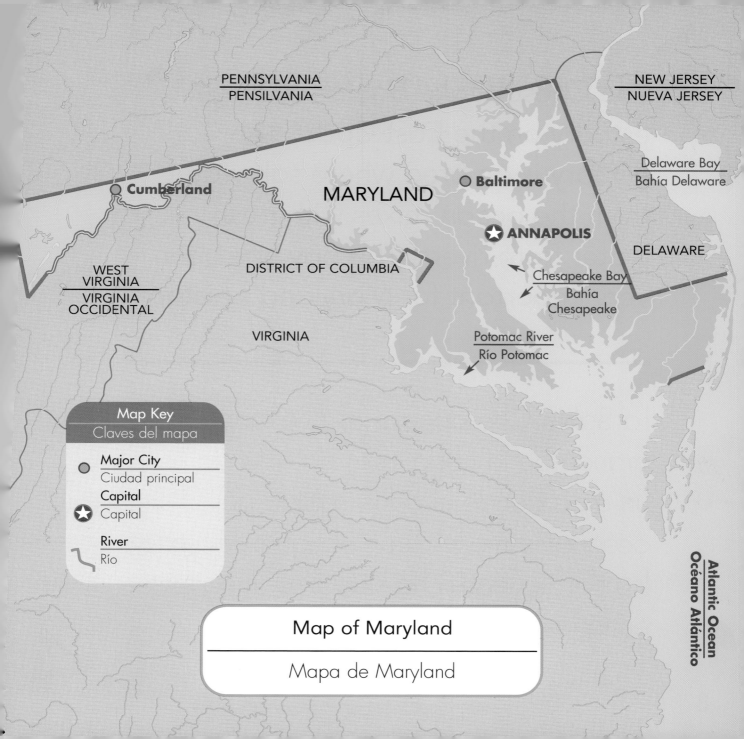

PENNSYLVANIA
PENSILVANIA

NEW JERSEY
NUEVA JERSEY

○ Cumberland

MARYLAND

○ Baltimore

Delaware Bay
Bahía Delaware

⭐ ANNAPOLIS

DELAWARE

WEST
VIRGINIA
VIRGINIA
OCCIDENTAL

DISTRICT OF COLUMBIA

Chesapeake Bay
Bahía
Chesapeake

VIRGINIA

Potomac River
Río Potomac

Map Key
Claves del mapa

○ **Major City**
Ciudad principal

⭐ **Capital**
Capital

River
Río

Atlantic Ocean
Océano Atlántico

Map of Maryland

Mapa de Maryland

The Chesapeake Bay is the largest estuary on the East Coast. An estuary is an area where salt water from the ocean mixes with fresh water from rivers. The bay has been very important for Maryland's history.

La Bahía Chesapeake es el estuario más grande de la costa este. Un estuario es un área donde el agua salada del océano se mezcla con el agua dulce de los ríos. La bahía ha sido muy importante en la historia de Maryland.

Sailboats at Chesapeake Bay

Veleros en la Bahía Chesapeake

Maryland History

Maryland was one of the 13 English colonies. George Calvert became the first Lord of Baltimore in 1632.

Historia de Maryland

Maryland fue una de las 13 colonias inglesas. En 1632, George Calvert se convirtió en el primer lord de Baltimore.

George Calvert, Lord of Baltimore

George Calvert, lord de Baltimore

Francis Scott Key wrote the poem that would later become our national anthem in Maryland. Key was inspired by watching Maryland soldiers guard the city of Baltimore in the War of 1812. The War of 1812 was fought against Great Britain.

Francis Scott Key escribió en Maryland el poema que, más tarde, se convertiría en el Himno Nacional de los Estados Unidos. Key se inspiró al ver marchar a los soldados de Maryland a defender la ciudad de Baltimore, durante la Guerra de 1812. La Guerra de 1812 fue contra Gran Bretaña.

Francis Scott Key

The first railroad company in the United States started in Baltimore, Maryland, in 1827. This railroad connected Baltimore with the state of Ohio.

La primera companía de ferrocarriles de los Estados Unidos se fundó en Maryland, en 1827. Este ferrocarril unió Baltimore con el estado de Ohio.

PETER COOPER'S "TOM THUMB" 1829-30 BALTIMORE & OHIO R. R.

America's First Train Engine in the Baltimore-Ohio Railroad

Primera locomotora americana del Ferrocarril Baltimore-Ohio

The Battle of Antietam was fought in Sharpsburg, Maryland. This was one of the Civil War's deadliest battles. More than 20,000 soldiers died in this battle. The Civil War was fought between the North and the South from 1861 to 1865.

La Batalla de Antietam se peleó en Sharpsburg, Maryland. Esta batalla fue una de las más sangrientas de la Guerra Civil. En esta batalla murieron más de 20,000 soldados. La Guerra Civil entre el Norte y el Sur tuvo lugar de 1861 a 1865.

Antietam Bridge, place of the Antietam Battle

Puente de Antietam, sitio de la Batalla de Antietam

Living in Maryland

Maryland is famous for its seafood, especially crabs. Fishermen have been fishing in the waters of Chesapeake Bay for years. Many Marylanders have fishing jobs.

La vida en Maryland

Maryland es famoso por sus pescados y mariscos, especialmente sus cangrejos. Sus pobladores han pescado en las aguas de la Bahía de Chesapeake por muchos años. Muchos marilandeses trabajan como pescadores.

Blue Crabs Being Harvested in Chesapeake Bay

Pesca de cangrejos azules en la Bahía Chesapeake

Annapolis, Maryland, has been the home of the U.S. Naval Academy since 1845. The academy trains men and women who want to work in the navy.

Annapolis, Maryland, ha sido el hogar de la Academia Naval de los E.U.A desde 1845. La academia entrena a los hombres y mujeres que desean trabajar en la marina.

Students at the U.S. Naval Academy

Estudiantes de la Academia Naval de E.U.A.

Maryland Today

High-technology companies are growing in Maryland.
High- technology companies make computer parts and programs, medicines, and airplanes.

Maryland, hoy

Muchas empresas de alta tecnología están surgiendo en Maryland. Las compañías de alta tecnología fabrican piezas y programas de computadoras, medicinas y aviones.

22

Working at the National Institutes of Health in Bethesda, Maryland

Trabajando en el Instituto Nacional de Salud en Bethesda, Maryland

Baltimore, Frederick, and Gaithersburg are important cities in Maryland. Annapolis is the capital of the state. The Maryland State House is the oldest capitol building in the country that is still in use.

Baltimore, Frederick y Gaithersburg son ciudades importantes de Maryland. Annapolis es la capital del estado. La Casa de Gobierno de Maryland es el capitolio más antiguo del país que aún continúa funcionando.

State House of Maryland in Annapolis
Casa de Gobierno de Maryland en Annapolis

Activity:
Let's Draw the Map of Maryland

Actividad:
Dibujemos el mapa de Maryland

1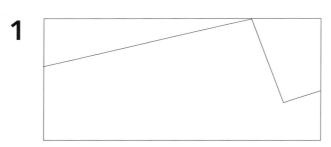

Start by drawing a horizontal rectangle. Use the rectangle as a guide and draw the sloping lines as shown.

Comienza por dibujar un rectángulo horizontal. Usando el rectángulo como guía dibuja las líneas inclinadas, como ves en el modelo.

2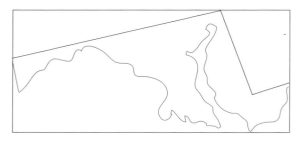

Draw the outline of the bottom half of the state.

Traza la forma de la parte inferior del estado.

3

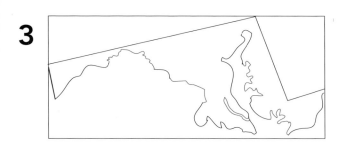

Now fill in more details along the border of the state. Erase the extra lines from step 2.

Agrega más detalles en la frontera del estado. Borra las líneas innecesarias del paso número 2.

Erase the rectangle guide and shade the drawing of Maryland. Draw a circle to mark Chesapeake Bay. Draw in a square to mark Baltimore. Use an *X* to mark the Antietam National Battlefield. Draw a star to mark Annapolis, the capital of Maryland.

4

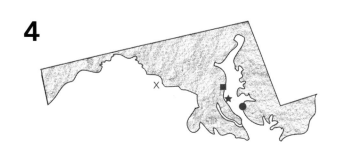

Borra el rectángulo que usaste como guía y sombrea el dibujo de Maryland.
Dibuja un círculo para marcar la Bahía de Chesapeake. Dibuja un cuadrado para marcar Baltimore. Usa una *X* para marcar el Campo Nacional de Batalla de Antietam. Dibuja una estrella en el lugar de Annapolis, la capital de Maryland.

Timeline   Cronología

Timeline		Cronología
Calvert leads the first English settlers to Maryland.	**1634**	Calvert guía hasta Maryland a los primeros colonos ingleses.
Slavery becomes legal in Maryland.	**1664**	La esclavitud se legaliza en Maryland.
British troops invade Baltimore.	**1814**	Tropas británicas invaden Maryland.
The Baltimore-Ohio Railroad begins construction.	**1844**	Comienza la construcción del Ferrocarril Baltimore-Ohio.
Samuel Morse demonstrates the telegraph by sending a message from Washington, D.C., to Baltimore.	**1862**	Samuel Morse inaugura el telégrafo enviando un mensaje desde Washington, D.C. a Baltimore.
The Battle of Antietam is fought in Sharpsburg.	**1862**	Se libra la Batalla de Antietam en Sharpsburg.
The Chesapeake Bay Bridge opens.	**1952**	Se inaugura el Puente de la Bahía Chesapeake.

Maryland Events

Eventos en Maryland

March
Winterfest in McHenry

April
Maryland Hunt Cup in Baltimore

May
Preakness Celebration in Baltimore

June
Bay County Music Festival
in Centerville
Tangier Sound Country Music Festival
in Crisfield

August
Montgomery County Agricultural Fair
Maryland State Fair at Timonium
National Hard Crab Derby
in Crisfield

October
St. Mary's Oyster Festival
in Leonardtown
Chesapeake Appreciation Day
Festival near Annapolis

December
Waterfowl Festival in Easton
Candlelight Tour of Havre de Grace

Marzo
Festival de invierno, en McHenry

Abril
Copa de cazadores Maryland, en Baltimore

Mayo
Celebraciones de Preakness, en Baltimore

Junio
Festival de música del Condado de Bay,
en Centerville
Festival de música country Tangier Sound,
en Crisfield

Agosto
Feria agrícola del Condado de Montgomery
Feria del estado de Maryland, en Timonium
Derby Nacional del cangrejo,
en Crisfield

Octubre
Festival de la ostra de St. Mary,
en Leonardtown
Festival del día del aprecio de Chesapeake,
cerca de Annapolis

Diciembre
Festival Waterfowl, en Easton
Gira de la candela de Havre de Grace

Maryland Facts/Datos sobre Maryland

English		Español
<u>Population</u> 5.2 million		<u>Población</u> 5.2 millones
<u>Capital</u> Annapolis		<u>Capital</u> Annapolis
<u>State Motto</u> Manly deeds, womanly words		<u>Lema del estado</u> Hechos masculinos, palabras femeninas
<u>State Flower</u> Black-eyed Susan		<u>Flor del estado</u> Rudbeckia Hirta
<u>State Bird</u> Baltimore Oriole		<u>Ave del estado</u> Oriol de Baltimore
<u>State Nickname</u> The Old Line State		<u>Mote del estado</u> El estado de la Vieja Línea
<u>State Tree</u> White Oak		<u>Árbol del estado</u> Roble blanco
<u>State Song</u> "Maryland! My Maryland!"		<u>Canción del estado</u> ""¡Maryland! ¡Mi Maryland!"

Famous Maryland /Marylandeses famosos

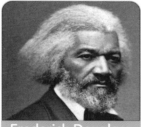

Frederick Douglass
(1817–1895)

Civil rights leader
Líder de los derechos civiles

Harriet Tubman
(1820–1913)

Abolitionist
Abolicionista

George "Babe" Ruth
Herman *(1895–1948)*

Baseball player
Jugador de béisbol

Helen Taussig
(1898–1986)

Scientist
Científica

Philip Glass
(1937–   )

Composer
Compositor

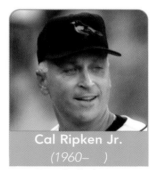

Cal Ripken Jr.
(1960–   )

Baseball player
Jugador de béisbol

Words to Know/Palabras que debes saber

border
frontera

coat of arms
blasones

railroad
ferrocarril

seafood
pescados y
mariscos

Here are more books to read about Maryland:
Otros libros que puedes leer sobre Maryland:

In English/En inglés:

My First Book About Maryland
The Maryland Experience
by Marsh, Carole
Gallopade International, 2000

The Maryland Colony (Our Thirteen Colonies)
by Williams, Jean Kinney and , Gilg, Eric
Child's World, 2003

Words in English: 322

Palabras en español: 353

Index

Índice